Female Fitness Stars of TV and the Movies

featuring profiles of
Cher, Goldie Hawn, Lucy Lawless,
and Demi Moore

Patricia Costello

Mitchell Lane Publishers, Inc.
PO Box 619
Bear, DE 19701

LEGENDS OF HEALTH & FITNESS

Role Models for Young Adults
Who Want to Lead a Healthy and Fit Lifestyle

Fitness Stars of the Martial Arts • Susan Zannos
1-58415-012-2
Bruce Lee, Chuck Norris, Carlos Machado, Cynthia Rothrock

Fitness Stars of Boxing • Phelan Powell
1-58415-013-0
George Foreman, Marvin Hagler, Oscar De La Hoya, Zulfia Koutdussova

Fitness Stars of Pro Football • John Torres
1-58415-014-9
Deion Sanders, Shannon Sharpe, Darrell Green, Wayne Chrebet

Fitness Stars of Pro Baseball • Ann Graham Gaines
1-58415-022-X
Brady Anderson, Mark McGwire, Ivan Rodriguez, Ken Griffey Jr.

Female Stars of Nutrition and Weight Control • Susan Zannos
1-58415-015-7
Marilu Henner, Suzanne Somers, Oprah Winfrey, Nadia Comaneci

Female Stars of Physical Fitness • Ann Graham Gaines
1-58415-023-8
Denise Austin, Christie Brinkley, Claudia Schiffer, Tyra Banks

Trailblazers of Physical Fitness • Phelan Powell
1-58415-024-6
Joe Weider, Jack LaLanne, Jake Steinfeld, Richard Simmons

Male Fitness Stars of TV and the Movies • Susan Zannos
1-58415-016-5
John Travolta, Sylvester Stallone, Wesley Snipes, Bruce Willis

Female Fitness Stars of TV and the Movies • Patricia Costello
1-58415-050-5
Demi Moore, Cher, Goldie Hawn, Lucy Lawless

Fitness Stars of Bodybuilding • John Torres
1-58415-051-3
Arnold Schwarzenegger, Lou Ferrigno, Ronnie Coleman, Lenda Murray

MITCHELL LANE PUBLISHERS, INC.

WHY DO WE CARE ABOUT HEALTH & FITNESS?

Do you remember the old adage that goes, "If you don't have your health, you have nothing at all?" When we are young, we think we are immortal. We think we are invincible. We will never get sick, grow old, or die. But, as we get older, we become more aware of our mortality. We realize that we can't enjoy life if we are not healthy. We can't go to work every day and earn a living. We get tired on short walks or winded walking up stairs. We are only on this earth for a short while, and to live life to its fullest, we must make sure we stay healthy and fit.

Healthy habits begin early in life. We need exercise and good nutrition every day. Millions of people have adopted daily workout routines and nutritious, healthy eating habits. Among these millions are some very famous people, who despite their very active lives, make time each day to ensure their health and fitness. They come from many different careers and backgrounds. In this series, we have put together profiles of forty fitness role models whose dedication to health and fitness complement their life and career. Hopefully, you will make the same commitment to health and fitness that these people have made and as a result, will enjoy a long, happy, and healthy life.

Mitchell Lane
PUBLISHERS

First Printing

Library of Congress Cataloging-in-Publication Data

Costello, Patricia, 1956-

      Female fitness stars of TV and the movies/Patricia Costello.

         p. cm.—(Legends of health & fitness)

      Filmography: p.

      Includes bibliographical references and index.

      Summary: Describes the lives and physical fitness routines of movie stars Demi Moore, Cher, Goldie Hawn, and Lucy Lawless.

      ISBN 1-58415-050-5

      1. Actresses—United States—Biography—Juvenile literature. 2. Physical fitness—Juvenile literature. [1. Actors and actresses. 2. Physical fitness.] I. Title. II. Series.

PN2285 .C67 2000

792'.028'092273—dc21

[B]   00-024431

About the Author: Patricia Costello has been an author and editor for more than 15 years. She holds degrees from San Francisco State University and the University of Southern California. She has authored numerous elementary, middle school, and high school textbooks, and also works as a reviewer for several publishers, reviewing various educational textbooks. She is an instructor of English at San Francisco City College.

Photo Credits: pp. 6, 21 Superstock; p. 22 Harry Langdon/Shooting Star; p. 26 Globe Photos; p. 28 The Kobal Collection; p. 32 Mark Allan/Globe Photos; p. 42 Ron Davis/Shooting Star; pp. 48, 52, 54 The Kobal Collection; p. 56 Archive Photos; p. 60 T. Ranz/Shooting Star; p. 65 Globe Photos; pp. 67, 71, 74 Shooting Star; p. 78 Archive Photos; p. 82 Ed Geller/Globe Photos; p. 90 The Kobal Collection

Acknowledgments: The following stories have been thoroughly researched and to the best of our knowledge, represent true stories. While every possible effort has been made to ensure accuracy, the publisher will not assume liability for damages caused by inaccuracies in the data, and makes no warranty on the accuracy of the information contained herein. None of the stories contained in this book have been authorized nor endorsed by the person being profiled.

Table of Contents

Physical fitness is essential for maintaining a healthy life.

CHAPTER ONE
Health & Fitness on TV
and at the Movies

Being healthy and fit has never been more important in the United States than it is today. Perhaps because people's lives have become busier and more stressful, we strive harder to stay in shape. Caught up in the national wave of physical fitness, more and more Americans are questioning their health regimens.

"Am I as fit as I'd like to be?" many people wonder. "Do I need to watch my diet?" "Should I join a health club?" "What steps do I need to take to be more physically attractive and feel better?" This concern with health and fitness has prompted millions of people to enroll in gyms, visit health food stores, run to juice bars, and buy more and more diet books and exercise videos. There is no doubt that over the past 20 years, health and fitness have become an essential way of life for many Americans. We not only want to look good but also to feel good as well.

Today many of us have jobs that require us to look and feel our best. We work long hours and have to take good care of ourselves. Often success on the job depends on this. We are often judged by our appearance not only to get a job but also to keep it and be promoted.

Of course, no one realizes more than people in the public eye how important appearance is. TV personalities and movie stars must always look and feel their best. Their livelihoods often depend on how youthful and fit they appear. Yet, they often have grueling work schedules. Actors may have to adapt their diet or exercise routines to prepare for roles that require certain body types. TV and movie stars know that every weight gain or loss—even a small amount—is constantly being scrutinized by the media, too.

Because of the tremendous pressure to look good, many stars employ the services of celebrity trainers. For example, talk-show host Oprah Winfrey hired personal trainer Bob Greene to help her lose 85 pounds and become fit enough to run in a marathon. Jennifer Aniston, star of *Friends*, crosstrains with Kathy Kaehler, who is a regular on the television show *Today* and author of the book *Real-World Fitness*. The routine she designed for Jennifer Aniston is simple, but rigorous: she works out for 15 minutes doing cardiovascular exercise (running or using stairclimber equipment), then weight trains for 45 minutes. Hobbies that also help keep her fit include mountain biking and yoga classes.

Celebrity trainer Harry Hanson of Manhattan, New York, has a contract with Paramount Pictures to train movie stars. At his fitness centers, Hanson customizes workouts for the individual. For naturally lean models like Naomi Campbell and Linda Evangelista, he focuses on toning their muscles with weights. For stars like Julia Roberts and Tyra Banks, who sometimes need to lose weight and keep it off, he prescribes regular cardiovascular work and a good diet.

Another popular young actress who also works out under the guidance of top trainers is Jennifer Lopez.

Trainer Radu Teoduoescu is impressed with Lopez's athleticism, "She could do anything. Mother Nature, you know?" Jennifer's fans are also aware of her natural athleticism. In an interview she once commented, "I was always into sports. I did gymnastics, competed nationally in track, and was on the school softball team." To prepare for her role in the film *Out of Sight*, Lopez sought the assistance of two fitness trainers, Nancy Kennedy and Bobby Strom, who helped her get in shape with an exercise routine involving weights, boxing, and water aerobics. Kennedy also designed Jennifer's diet, preparing high-protein, low-fat meals that helped her maintain her shapely figure. Since diet is as important as exercise to looking and feeling good, many stars like Lopez employ special cooks and consult nutritionists.

Actress Minnie Driver sought nutritional advice to prepare for her appearance in the movie *Circle of Friends*. For the part she was playing, Driver needed to gain 20 pounds. Later, of course, she had to lose that extra weight to get other parts. With the help of her trainer-nutritionist, Minnie was able to take off the weight in a short amount of time. Her current diet requires that she avoid white potatoes, bread, white rice, dairy, and sugar.

Actress Melanie Griffith, on the other hand, found that she had to lose a great deal of weight after the birth of her daughter. Soon after the baby was born, Griffith returned to her prepregnancy workout routine in order to speed up her metabolism rate. Along with the exercise program, Melanie eats small meals frequently and drinks shakes of soy-protein powder, apple juice, and bananas, prepared by her trainer-nutritionist.

How times have changed since the Hollywood days of 50 years ago. According to clothing designer Nolan Miller, "In the old days everybody drank hard liquor. Now you go to a cocktail party and everyone's got a little glass of white wine or mineral water." Miller has been designing outfits for women in Hollywood for a long time. For him, the old days were the 1950s. At that time, smoking was "cool" and a new style of cooking called TV dinners was becoming popular. Unfortunately, following these fads was not a very good way to stay healthy and fit.

Americans did have their own personal trainer during that time, though. His name was Jack LaLanne. At age 15, Jack began reading about the benefits of fitness on the human body. In 1936, at the age of 21, he opened the first modern health studio, in Oakland, California. LaLanne believed people should eat a healthy diet. According to him, everyone should be on low-fat, high fiber, no-sugar diets to stay in shape. Of course, LaLanne was espousing an idea decades before the concept became accepted by most Americans. Along with encouraging people to develop good eating habits, LaLanne established routines at his studio for people to work out with weights. At the time, though, medical doctors opposed the idea of this kind of exercise, saying it would give them heart attacks. LaLanne laughed at the notion and said that all the top bodybuilders weightlift, so why not everyone else?

From 1952 to 1986, LaLanne hosted a TV program during which he demonstrated exercises and promoted physical fitness. LaLanne himself was a phenomenal athlete. At age 41 he swam with his hands cuffed from Alcatraz Island to Fisherman's Wharf in San Francisco, California. At age 60 he repeated the same stunt, only this time he was not only handcuffed but also shackled and towing a thousand pound boat. Now in his eighties, Jack LaLanne is still working out. He travels worldwide, giving lectures about the benefits of regular exercise and good nutrition.

Of course, having a personal trainer and nutritionist can cost a great deal of money. The average person can't afford to hire this kind of help, and not all stars choose to consult health specialists. *Good Morning America*'s correspondents Cynthia McFadden, Sylvia Chase, and Diane Sawyer follow a program called "Lose Weight with *GMA*." Created for GMA by the National Institutes of Health, the trim-plan program encourages Americans to lose weight by dieting and working out with a partner or a group. This way they will be motivated to stay with the routine. Diane Sawyer also participates in television star Rosie O'Donnell's "Chub Club." This buddy-system fitness program, created by O'Donnell, sponsors a 5-kilometer run for its members to encourage them to get into shape. The Chub Club founder explains the goals of her program: "It's not about denying yourself. . . . it's about having fun."

For stars, getting and staying in good physical shape is nothing new. One of the first examples of a star who was in top physical condition was Johnny Weissmuller. As a teenager, Weissmuller was a champion swimmer. He won a total of five gold medals in the 1924 and 1928 Olympic games. Weissmuller got his start in films by appearing in several swimming documentaries. However, it was when he debuted in 1932 as the star of the film *Tarzan, the Apeman*, that Weissmuller's career really took off. Based on the novels of Edgar Rice Burroughs, the movie is about a strong, primitive man living in the jungles of Africa, capable of swinging from tree to tree on long jungle vines. Weissmuller went on to star in 12 more Tarzan films. In 1939 and 1940 he also performed in spectacular water shows called the Aquacade Revue, a musical performance of hundreds of swimmers, divers, singers, and special effects. Another famous swimmer, Esther Williams, costarred with Weissmuller in the Aquacade Revue.

Esther Williams was not just any swimmer, though; she was a swimming champion. She had earned a spot on the 1940 U.S. Olympic team and been headed for the games. However, the beginning of World War II canceled the Olympic games, and she couldn't prove herself there. Instead Williams became well-known for her film roles in swimming musicals from the early 1940s until the end of the 1950s. In her movies, she performed elaborate dance sequences involving diving and synchronized swimming. These films often incorporated a love story or some other theme, and had titles such as *Neptune's Daughter* (1949) and *Million Dollar Mermaid* (1952). What is remembered best about these movies, however, is Williams's top form as a swimmer. She was always graceful and feminine, as well as an incredible athlete. In contrast to the swimming performance films of the 1940s and 1950s, water sport programs today are full of action-packed sequences instead. Like the southern California–based TV show *Bay Watch*, these shows also may feature muscular, tanned sunbathers working out on the beach.

Because of the dramatic impact that sports events and athletic games can have, they often serve as a central theme in movies. Often the plots of sport-oriented films are interwoven with concepts of love and valor. For example, the British film drama *Chariots of*

Fire, which won the Oscar for Best Picture in 1981, is set during the 1924 Paris Olympic games. In this true story, a group of college athletes from England compete in the Olympic track and field events. Along the way they must deal with personal choices that challenge their integrity. An inspiring film, *Chariots of Fire* was described as two men chasing dreams of glory.

Another example of sport-oriented movies is the 1985 film *Vision Quest.* Matthew Modine stars as a high school student who wants to win the Washington State Wrestling Championship. He gives it his all as he trains for the meet. In addition, a love theme is woven into the film as Modine also tries to win the affection of a beautiful older artist.

A fictional high school is the setting for the 1986 film *Hoosiers.* In this inspiring film, Gene Hackman plays an experienced coach of a small-town, boys basketball team in Indiana. With the coach's help, the team improves and each member becomes better than he thought possible.

A real-life film that deals with basketball hopefuls is the 1994 documentary *Hoop Dreams.* The movie follows the lives of two inner-city "basketball phenoms" through their high school and college years. Both young men dream of playing in the NBA (National Basketball Association). In the course of the film, we see how the two develop physically and emotionally both on and off the court.

Without a doubt one of the most popular sports portrayed in the movies is boxing. More than 100 films based on this theme have been produced. Sports-biography movies have showcased such boxing stars as Muhammad Ali, Jack Dempsey, and Ray Mancini. One popular film is *Raging Bull* (1980), directed by Martin

Scorsese, which tells the true story of the darker side of boxer Jake LaMotta, who is portrayed as a fallen hero.

A more optimistic boxing film was released in 1976, starring a then-unknown actor named Sylvester Stallone, who had written his own screenplay about a down-and-out boxer named Rocky Balboa. The resulting movie, *Rocky*, quickly gained a popular following because it told the story of an athlete who was determined to triumph against impossible odds. In the film we see Rocky's determination to get himself in shape physically and regain his self-confidence as a fighter. It is his determination that enables him to overcome personal defeat. The attempt to overcome some kind of adversity has often been a theme in sports movies.

In more recent decades, stories about the martial arts have become central themes in movies. The most well-known martial artist in films was a physically small but agile man named Bruce Lee. Born in 1940 in San Francisco, California, to Chinese-American parents, Lee grew up in Hong Kong, where his parents returned a year after his birth. As an adult, Lee considered himself a martial artist first, and an actor second. Lee gave private martial arts lessons to other actors, but it was through his films that he became a hero and teacher to millions.

Lee is most remembered for the kung-fu films he made in Hong Kong. His most popular works were the 1972 films *Fist of Fury*, *Return of the Dragon,* and *Game of Death,* in which he performed a style of martial arts called jeet kune do. This style combined all the strong points of karate and tae kwon do. Lee also became known to many members of American TV audiences in the 1960s when he played the role of Kato in the *Green Hornet* series. A masked hero, the Green Hornet roamed through the city with his side-kick, Kato, fighting urban crime and defending its victims. For Lee, playing the avenger to the wrongly injured was a common role, which he performed often in his films. Lee was so popular that upon his death in 1973, some 25,000 people attended his funeral.

Following in Lee's footsteps was Jackie Chan, who is probably the biggest star in Asia today. Chan Kong Sang (his real name) was born in Hong Kong in 1954. Chan trained in the Peking Opera and became an acrobat. He also excelled in the martial arts, and got his start in the movies as a stuntsman. With the film *Drunken Master* (1978), Jackie Chan became a kung-fu star. Chan actually starred in the sequel to Bruce Lee's *Fist of Fury*. In it he plays a reluctant student who excels at kung-fu.

Another internationally known marital-arts action star is Belgian Jean Claude Van Damme. A former European Karate Champion, Van Damme starred in the 1987 film *Blood Sport*, which is the true story of the American ninja Frank Dux. From 1989 to 1994, Van Damme also starred in four kickboxing films. He is known for portraying action characters who have a violent nature.

In sharp contrast to the athleticism exhibited in the sports of swimming, track, basketball, boxing, and the martial arts is the physical effort and stamina required in the art of dance. Because dance is usually carried off gracefully, people sometimes forget that the performer, whether onstage or in films, needs a great deal of strength and stamina.

One of the most famous dancers to star in films was Gene Kelly, who began his movie career in the 1940s. Actually, Kelly had originally wanted to be a baseball player with the Pittsburgh Pirates. He instead turned his talents to dance. In his films, Kelly represents the common man. Wearing a sports coat and loafers, he dances athletic routines and performs amazing feats using lampposts and umbrellas. Kelly tried to invent dances that fit in with the camera and its movements, calling his style of dancing "cine-dancing." Two of his best loved films were released in 1951: *Singing in the Rain* and *An American in Paris*. Both films were musicals that showcased Kelly's incredible talent.

Kelly had been preceded by another well-known dancer named Fred Astaire. Born in 1899, Astaire began his career in vaudeville—stage entertainment that was popular in the beginning of the 1900s. Vaudeville incorporated song and dance routines. Fred Astaire differed from Kelly in both his style and his dress. This elegant performer performed his dance routines while wearing a top hat and tuxedo. From vaudeville, Astaire went on to perform in films. Two of his most famous dancing partners were his sister Adele Astaire and longtime dance partner Ginger Rogers. Although Fred Astaire's dance routines seemed effortless, they were actually the result of hours of rigorous work. With his style, grace, and flair, Fred Astaire earned high praises, including being described by the *New York Times* as the ultimate dancer.

While entertainment such as dance may deceive an audience because it appears easy to do, there is another form of entertainment that clearly requires incredible athletic ability: circus acrobatics. One of the earliest exhibits of physical strength and fitness were circus performances, which, in one form or another, have proven popular over the centuries. It was natural then that films about the circus world would attract 20th century moviegoers. Even the first films, which were silent, made use of this theme. Over the next few decades, several other circus-theme films followed, some better than others. One of the most well-known was the 1956 film *Trapeze*. In the movie, Burt Lancaster, who was actually married to a circus acrobat, portrays a former trapeze artist. He becomes lame after attempting and failing a triple somersault. Tony Curtis, who plays the son of an old friend, wants Lancaster to teach him the triple somersault routine. Italian actress Gina Lollabrigida plays another aerial acrobat. To perform the acrobatic routines used in the film required tremendous physical strength. Interestingly, all the actors in the film performed their own stunts.

Probably the movie star most renowned for his physical fitness is Arnold Schwarzenegger, who was born in Graz, Austria. The actor started his career as a bodybuilder, beginning his training while still a teenager in his native homeland. He had become fascinated with the sport after watching dedicated bodybuilders in a gym in a nearby town. During Schwarzenegger's military service, he competed in the Junior Mr. Europe bodybuilding competition, in which he received a perfect score of 300. Schwarzenegger went on to win many other bodybuilding titles. In 1968, after winning his first Professional Mr. Universe title, he was invited by American bodybuilding champion Joe Weider to train in the United States. Two years after arriving in America, Schwarzenegger starred in his first film, *Hercules in New York* (1970). He continued to compete in bodybuilding competitions during this time, winning the Mr. Olympia title for six years running before deciding to retire from competition in 1975. Although finishing with bodybuilding, his film career was just taking off. In 1977 he appeared in the documentary *Pumping Iron*, a film that focused on his competitions for Mr. Universe and Mr. Olympia titles. Schwarzenegger went on to star in many feature-length films, most notably *The Terminator* and *Conan the Barbarian*, in which he would demonstrate his incredible physical strength.

The famous Austrian bodybuilder became a U.S. citizen in 1983. A major promoter of physical fitness, he served as chairman of the President's Council on Physical Fitness and Sports from 1983 to 1993. During this time he traveled to all 50 states, at his own expense, to promote physical fitness for children. Schwarzenegger is also a major supporter of the Special Olympics, a nonprofit sports program of sports training and competition for individuals with mental retardation. The organization was started by the family of his wife, Maria Shriver. Always a role model, Schwarzenegger also became a major sponsor and organizer of the Inner-City Games, a program for urban youths to help keep them out of gangs, drugs, and trouble.

Schwarzenegger may be the most well-known bodybuilder in recent times, but there have been many others who have strived to attain his physique. Not to be ignored of course are women bodybuilders. One such female bodybuilder, Rachel McLish, starred in the 1984 film *Getting Physical*. The movie centers around a fictional bodybuilding contest for women. A year later, McLish also starred in *Pumping Iron II: The Women*. Like its predecessor, *Pumping Iron*, the film features a bodybuilding competition, although this time it is a female bodybuilding contest. Like many other physically fit movie stars, McLish also stars in an exercise video, *In Shape with Rachel McLish* (1995).

However, the pioneer of fitness videos is Jane Fonda, who in 1978, at age 40, surprised the public by demonstrating both her great physical shape and enthusiasm for educating women about how to improve their health. Fonda challenged the popular notion that women were "over the hill" once they reached middle age. In 1981 she came out with *Jane Fonda's Workout Book*, and on talk shows publicized the need for women to stay in shape. Some 20 years and several videos later, Fonda continues to push the value of physical fitness for women. Fitness expert Kathy Kaehler of *Good Morning America* describes Fonda as a ....woman who has a fabulous body, amazing muscle tone, and amazing endurance.

Many women over the age of 40 have been influenced by fitness icon Jane Fonda. Among them is model Lauren Hutton, 55, who says, "Women are just beginning at 40. At 50 you hit your power." When Tina Turner turned 50 in 1995, she said, "I can't say I feel 50, because the way my mother and grandmother looked when I was growing up is not happening anymore." Turner, who boasted she was as fit at age 50 as she had been at age 30, was also quoted as saying, "The body is a machine. You train it to do what you want it to do." Another amazing over-40 actress is Jane Seymour. Although age 44 and pregnant with twins, she was often out on the course, playing a round of golf. Surely, these women help debunk the idea that women are not able to stay in shape after a certain age.

Some of these women have stayed in shape by using exercise video routines—a multitude of such videos have been produced during the past decade. Over the years, numerous stars, models, and trainers have produced their own exercise videos according to their own themes. No matter the age level or focus of these exercise videos, there is one for everyone. Fonda has produced several videos, including *Sculpting Workouts—Abs, Buns, Thighs* (1995). Actress Debbie Reynolds developed an exercise video that focuses on routines geared for more mature adults. While, for much younger audiences, a Barbie doll comes to life and performs dance routines in the 1992 video *Dance! Workout with Barbie.* The doll's workout has been approved by the Aerobics and Fitness Association of America, and the popular music accompanying the video is performed by *Party of Five* star Jennifer Love Hewitt. As Americans now do their best to reach optimum health levels, all these videos have become popular with millions of consumers.

Whether seen in feature films or exercise videos, stars who are in top physical condition influence the people watching them. While not many have the time, money, or hired help, like the stars do, to invest in elaborate health programs, their success in achieving physical fitness nevertheless inspires many people to try to achieve the same thing. The following four chapters of this book tell the stories of four amazing actresses. These four women have maintained top physical condition over the years and, through their example, encourage all of us to become more physically fit.

Running is one way to stay physically fit.

The amazing Cher is in top physical shape.

CHAPTER TWO
Cher

Many people consider Cher to be the ultimate survivor. She came from a poor family, struggled to make it in show business, and had her share of personal difficulties. Today, an accomplished actress and singer, she amazes the public as she constantly reinvents herself. Now in her fifties, Cher is at the top of the pop charts, the oldest female rock star to have a number one hit in the rock era. Her unbelievable rise to stardom did not come easily, though.

Cher was born Cherilyn Sarkisian on May 20, 1946, in El Centro, California. Her mother, Georgia Holt, was 18 years old when Cher was born. Holt left her husband, John Sarkisian, a handsome Armenian truck driver when Cher was just a few months old. Sarkisian was battling with drug addiction and, not surprisingly, he and Holt had a tumultuous on-again, off-again relationship throughout the years. The two married and divorced twice and lived together a third time. While Cher was growing up, her mother would marry at least eight times.

When Cher was barely a toddler, financial circumstances forced Holt to place her daughter in a Catholic home run by nuns. Although Holt visited Cher at the home daily, when the mother had saved enough money to support her child, she had difficulty getting Cher back. Cher's sister Georganne says of this time,

"Mom freaked out. She remembers it as the most traumatic thing in her life."

Georgia Holt, despite her financial problems, did her best to raise her daughters. Cher remembers her mother being a great source of encouragement. In Cher's book *The First Time*, the performer speaks of the love and support her mother gave her as a child: "Whenever I was feeling defeated or excluded, my mother would say, 'If it doesn't matter in five years, it doesn't matter.' If I was heartbroken, she would tell me, 'You might not be the prettiest or the most talented, you might not be the smartest, but you're special.' I got that locked into my brain and I never forgot it."

Cher's sister Georganne was born in 1951. Her father was John Southall, an actor. Holt and Southall divorced five years later. Life continued to be difficult for the two sisters. To try to make ends meet, their mother worked as a model, movie extra, and waitress. Cher, who was five years older than Georganne, helped raise her younger sister. Georganne remembers growing up in a poor household. "Mom sweated bullets every year figuring out how to get us new shoes for school," says Georganne. "We came from no money."

Cher describes her home life as chaotic. Despite her mother's multiple marriages, Cher says her mother managed to instill in her daughters the basic rule of honesty and helping other people when they are in trouble. Things changed for the family when Holt married Gilbert La Piere in 1961. A bank vice president, La Piere adopted both girls and gave them an upper-middle class lifestyle in Encino, California.

Early on, Cher decided she wanted to become famous. She watched TV shows that were popular during the '60s and decided she would like to be a television personality. TV, she thought, was a place you could become famous just by being friendly. From the age of 11, she practiced signing her autograph. She says she did it over and over again because she was sure one day she would need the experience. And always it was simply Cher. With her mother's many marriages, Cher's last name kept changing, and no one ever called her by her real first name—Cherilyn.

By age 16 Cher had become a little more sophisticated about how to succeed in the film and television business. She began studying acting and set out to make her mark. She dropped out of high school and moved into a Hollywood apartment with a girlfriend.

One day in 1963, Cher was in a coffee shop that many music industry people visited. She and her boyfriend at the time were supposed to be double dating with Cher's roommate and a friend of Cher's boyfriend. The friend was a 27-year old backup singer named Salvatore Phillip Bono, or Sonny Bono. He was an aspiring songwriter, who worked as a promoter for rock producer Phil Spector. Cher's boyfriend and roommate didn't dance, but Sonny and Cher did, and they ended up dancing and talking the whole night.

The two started out as friends, but with time their love grew. In 1964 they made up their own wedding ceremony by exchanging rings, but they legally married in 1969. Also in 1964 Sonny arranged for the young Cher to sing backup for a group called The Ronettes. And Sonny and Cher established themselves as singers known as Caesar and Cleo. Sonny had always said Cher reminded him of Cleopatra.

They soon released their first record, but it didn't hit the charts. Then they changed their name to Sonny and Cher. They also changed their look. They wore bell

Sonny and Cher were a hit in the 1960s.

bottom pants, a style popular in that era. They also wore colorful clothing and love beads. In July 1965 they recorded a song, "I Got You Babe," that Sonny had written. It went to number one on the charts and became a classic song of the 1960s. Its success—it sold more than 4 million copies—made them instant headliners. The couple released five more singles that year and played at major rock concerts throughout the

United States and Europe. Cher's dream of stardom was fulfilled.

Cher was an advocate for living a healthy life. She and husband Sonny made government-funded, anti-drug films. Their stance on drugs certainly went counter to the behavior of many rock stars of the time. The Beatles and The Rolling Stones used drugs and sang about their experiences, but that was not the style of Sonny and Cher. She was once quoted as saying, "I just have the feeling that people can't cope with drugs. If they could, it would be a different story. But I don't know anyone who can handle them. Drugs handle people, not the other way around." Because the '60s were a time of so much drug use, Sonny and Cher's popularity with their fans plummeted. Hard rock became popular. Acid rock groups were in, and Sonny and Cher were out.

To make a living, the two began performing in nightclubs. Cher, who admits to having chronic stage fright, says that at the time she was running on fear. She also adds that she learned from those years that you take your terror and you do whatever needs doing.

Cher definitely had to face that fear when she and Bono went on the nightclub circuit. When they were on the road, they had to face some tough crowds. Often they would be heckled by loud, obnoxious drunks in the audience. It was during this time that the two developed their comedy style. They would respond to the crowd by throwing insults back to the audience. Then they started teasing each other.

Their routines were noticed and, in 1971, they appeared in their own variety show series, *The Sonny and Cher Comedy Hour*. Their daughter Chastity, born in 1969, often appeared on the show with them. The show lasted until 1974 and the Bono's marriage until 1975. Bono had managed the couple professionally for their entire time together. Cher eventually found her husband too controlling and wanted to set out on her own.

The end of her marriage to Bono was the beginning of a difficult period in Cher's life. She married Greg Allman, a member of the rock band The Allman Brothers. At the time he was battling drug addiction problems. Their marriage lasted from 1975 to 1977. Son Elijah Blue was born in 1976.

After the divorce, Cher tried to make a musical comeback as a solo artist. She experimented with fully-orchestrated studio sound on the 1977 album *I'd Rather Believe in You* and then turned to disco in 1978 with *Take Me Home*. Neither album was very successful. In

In the film Mask, Cher plays opposite Sam Elliott as a mother coping with a disfigured son.

1980 she tried to form a hard rock band called Black Rose. It turned out to be a disaster with the critics.

On the positive side, Cher's nightclub venues in Las Vegas were selling out. She definitely had a flair for the stage. That's probably why she then decided to head for New York to try her hand at acting. At 35, an age when most actresses see a slump in their careers, Cher was taking a chance at becoming an actor. This was a brave move on her part, especially considering that years earlier, she and husband Sonny Bono had made two films, *Good Times* and *Chastity,* that flopped. The ever-adventurous Cher, however, was about to surprise everyone with her talent.

In describing her move to New York, Cher says, "I had no real confidence or faith that I'd succeed there. I did it with willpower. There was nothing else for me to do."

Cher did in fact succeed. She first appeared on the stage in the role of Sissy, a small town sexpot in the Broadway play *Come Back to the Five & Dime, Jimmy Dean, Jimmy Dean.* Cher went on to play the same part in the movie version in 1982.

When Cher was on the stage in New York, film director Mike Nichols noticed her talents. He asked her to take a part in his 1983 film *Silkwood.* In the movie, she plays a lesbian working in a plutonium plant and, uncharacteristic of Cher, wears very little make-up and very plain clothes. At first the flamboyant actress didn't like the part, but she eventually accepted the offer. After the film's release, critics acclaimed her performance. For her role in *Silkwood,* she was nominated for an Oscar and won the Golden Globe Award for Best Supporting Actress.

In the 1985 film *Mask,* Cher played the mother of a son who is disfigured with a craniofacial disorder.

For her performance in the film, many viewers thought she should have received an Oscar at the Academy Awards for Best Actress, but that honor did not come. After starring in *Mask,* Cher became involved in the Children's Craniofacial Association. As their honorary chairperson, she came up with the idea of creating a camp for children with craniofacial abnormalities. The first retreat was held in Florida and hosted by Disney. The second was hosted by Universal Studios and Sea World. Other cities that participated in following years were Phoenix, Indianapolis, Boston, Chicago, San Diego, and Dallas. Cher comments about her involvement with the group: "I love doing my work and in order to do your work, you have to look good. And when I measure this with these kids having to worry about just getting through the day without getting made fun of and when I think of these mothers whose hearts are torn out fifty million times a year. . . . I've been with these parents and given them pep talks because they are going through something I'll never have to go through. What I do seems so small, so nothing."

In 1987 Cher starred in three films—*The Witches of Eastwick, Suspect* and *Moonstruck.* For her performance in *Moonstruck,* she finally got her Oscar for Best Actress. In the film, she plays a Brooklyn Italian-American who falls in love with a baker. Cher jokes that even though she now uses the Oscar for a doorstop for her bedroom, she means no disrespect.

In 1990 Cher starred in the film *Mermaids.* It was about this time that a battle with chronic fatigue syndrome, or Epstein Barr, began. She had first been diagnosed with the illness in 1986, but it was not until about three years later that the symptoms hit hard. The disease often made her sick and left her with no energy.

Cher took several steps to try to overcome these symptoms. First, she took homeopathic remedies and, as she explained in a 1992 interview, "It was rough. My doctor put me on Japanese and German herbs and massive amounts of vitamin C." She also consulted with Robert Haas, a sports nutrition expert. Haas had advised such world-renowned athletes as tennis stars Ivan Lendl and Martina Navratilova.

Cher first met Haas in 1985, when she told him about her symptoms. In the year of grueling work filming *Mask*, she had gotten little sleep and had developed poor eating habits. Haas redesigned Cher's diet-and-exercise routine, developing a "Forever Fit Plan" for her. Cher says the plan helped her get through the next year, which was the most demanding time of her life. Besides making three films that year, she recorded an album, made two videos, and launched a fragrance line for women. She also sat for hundreds of interviews and did countless commercials and TV appearances. Later in 1991 Cher came out with a diet book, *Forever Fit*, that she cowrote with Haas. The book gives specific menus and exercise tips.

In 1991, at age 44, the busy actress did not slow down much. She was following a schedule that ran from 8 A.M. to 8 P.M. Cher claims that good health resulting from her dedication to fitness allowed her to follow such a demanding schedule.

When Cher hit her forties, she became a spokesperson for health and fitness. She came out with an exercise video called *Cherfitness: A New Attitude*, led by trainer Keli Roberts. It encouraged women to stay in shape through a three-part program that involves a 38-minute aerobic step workout, a 10-minute back muscle workout, and a 32-minute workout to shape hips, buns,

Cher's great voice has kept her popular with her fans for several decades.

and thighs. The video sold over a million copies in 1992 and prompted producers to launch another video called *Cherfitness: Body Confidence*. This video features aerobic dance led by Dori Sanchez, who choreographs all of Cher's live performances. It also includes weight-resistance training led by Karen Andes-Carcamo, an expert on the subject.

In making her first video Cher learned how many of her previous exercise habits were unhealthy. Her former workout routine had included twists and bends, exercises that were now banned by the AFAA (Aerobics and Fitness Association of America). For years she had done spine-twisting sit-ups and hyperextended kick-backs. An article in *American Fitness* magazine notes that it was amazing to find Cher still walking. In fact, the star did suffer from backaches.

Cher's old routine incorporated many bad exercise habits developed during the '60s and '70s: extremely high repetitions, and moves that caused excessive joint wear and tear. Before putting together a fitness video, Cher realized that her current exercise routine hadn't changed for more than 12 years and that some things would probably need updating.

To make sure her video was up-to-date, Cher reviewed tapes and classes of AFAA-certified instructors, and her exercise companion, Angela, attended an AFAA workshop. Angela studied and retooled her style and philosophy. Cher concurrently interviewed many trainers and selected a program she wanted to feature.

Cher loves to crosstrain. In *Ladies Home Journal* in 1991 she also stated that she thinks walking is the single most important exercise you can do. She says she tried running for years and hated it.

Cher kept busy for the next few years promoting health and fitness. Soon she was busy with other things as well. In 1993 some people approached her about going to Armenia. At that time inhabitants of the country were still recovering from a 1988 earthquake and were at war with the Azerbaijanis. By helping the people of Armenia, Cher could attract some publicity about how bad the situation was.

Cher's plane was loaded with supplies: medicine, clothing, toys, and food for the Armenians. In Armenia, Cher visited many private homes, where she described the people as gracious and kind. She also visited the orphanages, which were full of children whose parents had been killed in the fighting. There she helped distribute toys to the children. Cher described this trip as the strangest, most difficult, but most rewarding she had ever taken.

In 1996 Cher's career took another turn. Cher directed a segment of HBO's project *If These Walls Could Talk,* a trilogy about abortion. In describing her interest in directing, Cher states, "There's a place for me to make my talent visible. I don't know if it's in front or behind the camera, but I know I can contribute." *If These Walls Could Talk* got the highest ratings ever achieved at the time for an original HBO movie. Cher said, "It was so exciting for me—there was a unbelievable amount of satisfaction. Whenever you try something new, there's always the chance that you're going to be embarrassing. But I was better than I thought I'd be. Not as good as I'd like to be, but I'm on my way."

In addition to her career, Cher also has two children to whom she is devoted. Her daughter Chastity, whom she refers to as Chas gave her quite a surprise in the late 1980s. At age 19, Chastity came out as a lesbian. Cher says it was really difficult for her to accept that her daughter was gay. The two got into a big fight about it, but Cher says she finally came to terms with it. She and her daughter don't have any secrets anymore, and Chastity knows that her mother is always there for her.

Cher also had to cope with her son Elijah's rebellious period. At one point he was wearing women's clothing. Cher responded by saying that her son was just trying out a new look for his band. Elijah plays guitar with a rock group. He was into the "glam rock" look at the time, according to her. Cher notes that her son is extremely intelligent and talented. Cher says she is the first person her children call in a crisis and that she is proud of them both.

In January of 1998 Cher received what was probably the worst news in her life. Her ex-husband Sonny Bono had been killed in a skiing accident. Cher describes Sonny as having filled at one time or another every role she needed in her life—father, brother, mentor, husband, partner. In the beginning he was her rock. He understood her dreams to be someone different, an artist.

A longtime friend asked her to deliver his eulogy. At the end of her speech she said, "Son had always reminded me of a section in *Reader's Digest* that I used to read when I was young: 'The Most Unforgettable Character I ever Met.' For me that person was Salvatore Philip Bono." Cher says giving the eulogy was her toughest performance ever. "I had no control. My face was making all kinds of movements, I had to lock my legs and grit my teeth. I was terrified." Cher was careful to present her ex-husband in a good light. "I felt I had to repair all the damage and misconceptions about Sonny." Sonny Bono played the fool on their TV show, but Cher is careful to note that it was just part of the couple's act.

By the time Sonny died Cher's life had changed dramatically. She had turned fifty. "I hate my fifties," she says. "They suck. I never felt older until I hit 50. And the way I first noticed was through my work. When I was 40, I was playing opposite somebody who was 21, and nobody noticed. But at 45, as you start to look older, all you can do is look good for your age." Cher has managed to look good and stay in shape despite her 50 plus years and continues to amaze the public.

In 1999 fans saw her in yet another film, costarring with Dames Judi Dench, Joan Plowright and Maggie Smith in Franco Zeffirelli's *Tea with Mussolini.*

What's next for this amazing star? Cher will certainly continue to act and sing. She still performs in New York, Las Vegas, and Atlantic City nightclubs. *Time* magazine commented that whatever medium she chooses, Cher will continue "to woo the world through performance."

As a teen idol during the 1960s, Cher had symbolized the youthful, hip look that all young girls of the time tried to imitate. Now in her fifties, she still manages to maintain a youthful and healthy appearance that many want to copy. Like all actresses she must stay in great shape.

Infamous for her Bob Mackie–designed outfits, she has toned down her look somewhat. She says she is not as into fashion, the quantity of it, as she used to be.

Less shopping leaves more time for daily morning workouts and for designing a new 14,000 square-foot, seven-bedroom house overlooking the ocean in Malibu, California.

She is also having laser treatments to remove her colorful tattoos. "When I got them, no one else had them," says Cher. "Now everyone has them. They're not so fabulous anymore."

Most amazing is the fact that at age 52, she managed to ascend to the top of the pop charts again. With the release of her song "Believe," in 1999, Cher holds the record for having the longest gap of time between number one hits in the rock era. She also holds the record for having the longest span of time between number one hits: 33 years from "I Got You Babe" to "Believe."

Chronology

1946 Born Cherilyn Sarkisian, on May 20, to John Sarkisian and Georgia Holt Sarkisian, in El Centro, California

1964 Sings backup with Sonny Bono's group, The Ronettes

1965 Sonny and Cher launch career with "I Got You Babe"

1969 Marries Sonny (Salvatore Philip) Bono

1969 Daughter Chastity Bono is born

1971–1974 Stars in television variety series with husband Sonny Bono in *The Sonny and Cher Comedy Hour*

1973 Receives Golden Globe Award for Best Actress in a Television Series (Comedy or Musical) for *The Sonny and Cher Show*

1975 Divorces Bono and marries rock star Greg Allman

1976 Son Elijah Blue Allman is born

1977 Divorces Greg Allman

1983 Nominated for an Academy Award for Best Supporting Actress for *Silkwood;* receives Golden Globe Award for Best Supporting Actress, *Silkwood*

1988 Wins Academy Award for Best Actress for her role in *Moonstruck*

1999 Song "Believe" becomes number one hit on the pop charts

2000 Wins Grammy for "Believe"

Filmography

1965   *Wild on the Beach*

1967   *Good Times*

1969   *Chastity*

1982   *Come Back to the Five and Dime, Jimmy Dean,*
       Jimmy Dean

1983   *Silkwood*

1985   *Mask*

1987   *Moonstruck*

1987   *Suspect*

1987   *The Witches of Eastwick*

1990   *Mermaids*

1992   *The Player*

1994   *Ready to Wear (Prêt-à-Porter)*

1996   *Faithful*

1999   *Tea with Mussolini*

Books

Forever Fit: The Lifetime Plan for Health
Beauty
The First Time

Discography
(Selected Hits–Albums and Singles)

1965 *All I Really Want to Do*

1965 *I Got You Babe*

1965 *Baby Don't Go*

1965 *Look at Us*

1966 *Cher*

1966 *The Sonny Side of Cher*

1966 *The Wondrous World of Sonny & Cher*

1967 *The Best of Sonny & Cher*

1967 *Good Times*

1967 *In Case You're in Love*

1967 *With Love, Cher*

1968 *Cher's Golden Greats*

1968 *With Love, Backstage*

1969 *3614 Jackson Highway*

1971 *All I Ever Need Is You*

1971 *Gypsies, Tramps and Thieves*

1971 *Sonny & Cher Live*

1972 *All I Ever Need Is You*

1972 *Cher's Greatest Hits*

1972 *Cher Superpak, Volumes I and II*

1972 *Foxy Lady*

1972 *The Two of Us*

1973 *Half-Breed*

1973 *Live in Las Vegas, Volume II*

1973 *Mama Was a Rock and Roll Singer*

1974 *Bittersweet White Light*

1974 *Dark Lady*

1974 *Greatest Hits*

1975 *Stars*

1976 *Allman and Woman: Two the Hard Way*

1979 *Take Me Home*

1981 *Best of Cher, Volumes I and II*

1982 *I Paralyze*
1985 *Golden Greats*
1989 *At Their Best*
1990 *Bang Bang, My Baby Shot Me Down*
1991 *The Beat Goes On—The Best of Sonny and Cher*
1991 *Love Hurts*
1992 *Bang Bang & Other Hits*
1992 *Extravaganza: Live at the Mirage*
1996 *It's a Man's World*
1996 *One by One*
1996 *Paradise is Here*
1999 *Strong Enough*
1999 *All or Nothing*
1999 *Believe*
2000 *20th Century Masters*

Television

1971–74	*The Sonny and Cher Comedy Hour* (series)
1975–76	*Cher* (series)
1976–77	*The Sonny and Cher Show* (series)
1983	*Cher—A Celebration at Caesar's Palace* (special)
1991	*Cher. . . At the Mirage* (special)
1996	*If These Walls Could Talk* (performer, segment director)

*Goldie Hawn looks better in her fifties than many women do in their twenties.
A lot of her good looks are attributed to her passion for fitness.*

CHAPTER THREE
Goldie Hawn

"People asked me what I wanted to be when I grew up," Goldie Hawn remembers. "And I'd say, 'Happy.' That was all I wanted to be." The bubbly blonde actress, producer, and mother has managed to maintain this attitude throughout her life while fulfilling her personal and professional goals.

Goldie Jean Hawn was born in Takoma Park, Maryland, on November 21, 1945. She was the younger daughter of Edward Rutledge Hawn and Laura Speinhoff Hawn. Sister Patti was seven years older. Edward Hawn was a violinist and Laura Hawn was the owner of a dance school. The couple had met in 1929, at the beginning of the Great Depression.

Goldie's parents came from two different worlds: Edward was a Protestant musician from Arkansas and Laura was a Jewish jewelry wholesaler from Pittsburgh. Both of their families worried whether the interfaith marriage would succeed. Laura's family was also concerned about her marrying someone with such an unstable profession—working in the music business. Nonetheless, the two married. By day the couple ran a jewelry store and watch repair shop. At night Edward played music in a band.

Eventually the Hawns' hard work paid off. After the birth of their daughter Patti in 1937, Edward became very much in demand and worked in high-profile orchestras in the Washington, D.C. area. Laura Hawn had left the jewelry business and opened a dance studio, the Roberta Fera School of Dance, in partnership with a local dance instructor. It was into this artistic family that Goldie Hawn was born.

Edward Hawn, who could trace his ancestors back to the youngest signer of the Declaration of Independence, had a strong influence on his younger daughter. He was always there to give Goldie advice and guidance. "My father always kept me on the straight and narrow in terms of what was real and what wasn't. He said, 'If you think you're too big for your britches, just go stand in the ocean and feel how small you really are.' I always remember that," the actress says.

Hawn grew up in a household full of music and dance. It was as a dancer that she got her start in show business. As a young girl Hawn received lessons not only in dance but also in voice, piano, and acting. Her mother, who Hawn insists was not a stage mother, encouraged Goldie to develop her talents. At the age of 10, she danced with the chorus of a local production of *The Nutcracker Suite,* along with the well-known Ballet Russe de Monte Carlo.

Goldie's early training as a dancer helped form her determination to succeed. She says she learned one of her most important lessons at the age of 12 when she performed at a friend's bar mitzvah. When she started her routine, she slipped and fell. She got up, calmed herself, and when the music started again, fell a second time. Finally, on the third try, she succeeded. "I realized I was probably the little girl who was going to make it," she remembers. At that young age Hawn could see it takes a strong belief in oneself and perseverance to succeed in life.

At age 17, Hawn turned her love of dance into a profession. She opened Goldie's Dancing School, where she was known as a kind, patient, and encouraging teacher. Hawn remembers fondly her teaching days and says that if she hadn't made it in show business, she would have been quite happy to teach the rest of her life. In 1963, Hawn enrolled at American University in Washington, D.C. as a drama major.

In Washington, Hawn auditioned for roles in local theater groups that would allow her to improve her acting skills. She appeared in a summer run of *Romeo and Juliet* and got great reviews. It was then that she decided to head for New York and try to make it in show business. During the next few years, Hawn had a rough time getting jobs as a dancer. Jobs were hard to come by and Hawn resorted to taking jobs as a go-go dancer, then a popular type of dancing. Go-go dancing involved dancing in cages and on tabletops in front of rowdy, drunken men. Hawn was defensive of her decision to become a go-go dancer, explaining, "I had to make a buck, you know? So I hooked up with this go-go dancing agent on Sixth Avenue and would go down there when things got tight and say, 'Do you have anything for me today?'"

In 1966 a choreographer suggested that Hawn move to the West Coast and work in tent musicals there. Sick of New York by this time, Goldie picked up and headed west. However, she had difficulties finding employment in California as well. She was ready to give up when suddenly her luck changed. TV personality Andy Griffith was hosting a TV special, and Hawn got a chance to audition for a dance part. At the audition she was spotted by an agent for the high-power William Morris Agency, and she finally got her start.

Hawn got her next TV role in a comedy series called *Good Morning World*. The show ran from 1967 to 1968. Always exuberant, Hawn was hired next in the role of "Giggly Girl" for the 1968 movie *The One and Only, Genuine, Original Family Band*. In this role, she played a dancer and, as the name suggests, was very lighthearted. These roles were the beginning of Hawn's career in comedy. Next, veteran comedians Rowan and Martin noticed her and her distinctive giggle, which helped her land a job on the late '60s comedy show *Laugh-In*. In this comedy revue series, she played the wide-eyed dizzy blonde who hammed it up to the camera and wore body paint and psychedelic daisies on her cheeks.

The show *Laugh-In* often spoofed the politics of the time, such as the unpopular war in Vietnam. Hawn was one of a lineup of comedians who performed crazy antics and delivered zany lines to the audience. Goldie became famous saying the line "Sock it to me," after which she was usually splashed with water. While the series ran, Hawn was twice nominated for Emmys for her performances in the slapstick show.

However, after spending two-and-a-half years on *Laugh-In*, Hawn decided she wanted more opportunities. She tried out for a part in the film *Cactus Flower* and won the role of Walter Matthau's naive girlfriend. In 1969 she won an Oscar for Best Supporting Actress for her performance in the film. That same year she married dancer and director Gus Trikonis. They divorced five years later.

In 1976 Hawn married her second husband, actor Bill Hudson. The couple had two children: son Oliver

Hudson and daughter Kate Hudson. Hawn and Hudson divorced in 1979.

The '70s saw Hawn in many more films. She starred in an off-beat romantic comedy with Peter Sellers in the 1970 film *There's a Girl in My Soup*. In a 1972 release, *Butterflies Are Free*, she played an oddball actress who befriends a blind neighbor in Greenwich Village, New York. Then, in 1975, she played one of the many girlfriends of a womanizing hairdresser (Warren Beatty) in *Shampoo*. Beatty was the first man in Hollywood to tell her that she was smart.

Despite all the "dumb blonde" roles she has played, Goldie Hawn is really a talented actress and a shrewd businesswoman. Her career spans thirty years and includes more than two dozen films in which she has acted, produced, or directed. Actually, Hawn started out her acting career by studying Shakespeare and has had a great deal of professional training. However, although the comedian has taken some dramatic roles, most people wouldn't remember them. In her words, "I'm smarter than people give me credit for. I have a light personality and a deep-thinking brain. Those are two different things."

In 1980 Hawn starred in *Private Benjamin* as a spoiled rich girl who goes to military "boot camp." Hawn not only played the lead but also was the movie's executive producer.

Benjamin was a role that definitely required being physically fit. Hawn, with the cooperation of the U.S. Army, went through six weeks of basic training in late 1979 and early 1980, at Fort MacArthur, California. She experienced the physical rigors of basic training and endured the drill sergeant's screaming in her face. In the film, Hawn has to crawl through the mud and climb over high embankments. She has to with-

Hawn endures the physical rigors of Army life in Private Benjamin.

stand the tough sergeant's severe punishments such as endless push-ups and latrine duty—not the kind of activities for someone who is out of shape.

Hawn says she wanted to produce *Private Benjamin* so she could call her own shots while making the film. With this one producing credit, Hawn decided to team up with costume designer Anthea Sylbert to form the Hawn/Sylbert Movie Company. Such a move was considered risky, but the versatile star helped pave the way for other women to become film producers. After *Private Benjamin* Hawn produced five more films.

A few years after *Private Benjamin* was released, Hawn was casting for roles in her next film, *Swing Shift.* In this dramatic film, she plays a navy wife who takes an assembly-line job at a World War II munitions plant, where she falls in love with a fellow worker. Goldie was looking for someone to play opposite her when actor Kurt Russell tried out for the part. He asked her at the time if she remembered him from the time they had first met—in 1968, on the film set of *The One and Only, Genuine, Original Family Band.* At that time Russell was 16 and Hawn was about 21. Hawn says he was, of course, too young for her at the time. She had noted that he was very cute and she did remember him. The two hit it off and began dating. They have been together since 1983. Their son Wyatt was born in 1986.

Hawn says family is her first priority. "Motherhood is everything to me," she states. She wants to feel that her children are on the right footing, that they feel solid about themselves, and that they find out what they want to do in life. The Hawn-Russell household includes son Wyatt, Goldie's two children—Oliver and Kate Hudson—from her previous marriage, and Boston—Kurt's son from a previous marriage. They make their home in Los Angeles.

It's a pretty busy family. In addition to Goldie's many career responsibilities, she is a very active mom. She keeps up on all the children's activities. Her son Wyatt is a star goalie. Russell's son Boston is a student at Georgetown University. Oliver and Katie Hudson are both aspiring actors. Oliver played Goldie's son in her 1999 movie, *The Out-of-Towners.* Katie was in the movie *200 Cigarettes,* with Ben Affleck and Courtney Love. Daughter Katie was also in an episode of the television show *Party of Five.* Hawn says her house is like the Actors' Studio. The two children are always rehearsing scripts.

Hawn says she and her daughter talk all the time about the pros and cons of acting. They discuss what it's like being in the public eye. Hawn says, however, that she would be thrilled if her daughter became known as a great actor.

Hawn says, "The key to raising children is mutual respect and admiration . . . but there must also be standards . . .of right and wrong. I don't let my children curse in this house. That's something I've always been a real stickler about. I don't like bad language. Period. Not allowed."

The fun-loving Goldie naturally likes to have fun with her family. Hawn describes one family trip fondly: "We laughed and sang all the way." Her son Oliver said to her, "Mom, I have the most fun with our family. We laugh more than anybody."

Hawn says her children love for her to cook. She thinks she's a pretty good chef. When the family is together at their ranch in Aspen, Colorado, Goldie says she cooks all the time. Getting the family to sit down together is another matter. With everyone's busy schedules, it's hard to get them all seated at the table at the same time. Hawn says that every Sunday she makes dinner. Her friends come over and, if they want, her kids bring their friends.

Hawn was also especially close to her mother. After Laura Hawn suffered a heart attack, Kurt and Goldie took her into their home and cared for her themselves. Hawn put her career on hold until after her mother's death in 1993. Hawn says having her mother living with them at their home was a good experience for her children. "They had an opportunity to live with their grandmother, which I think is very important," she says.

Hawn describes losing her mother as the hardest thing she has ever gone through. In terms of real-life roles, she ranks being a daughter as most important, then a mother, and last, an actor. When her mother was alive, Goldie would perform for her. When she died, Goldie says she had nobody to perform for except herself. Hawn says she has a very strong work ethic. But after her mother died, Goldie didn't want to go back to work. Instead, she did a lot of traveling and spiritual work.

Hawn views her spirituality as part of her health routine. She was raised in the Jewish faith, but not in a strict religious atmosphere. She is now a Buddhist and has incorporated 20 minutes of meditation into her daily routine. Hawn feels that this practice keeps her centered. She tells people that it is important to spend a few moments in quiet solitude. She believes it helps rejuvenate the brain cells. Hawn also contends that a calm face—one that is without stress—is a younger face.

In 1996 Hawn returned to filmmaking with the release of the comedy *First Wives Club*, in which she

Hawn makes a comeback in The First Wives Club.

played a fading Hollywood star. Hawn described her character as "over the top—the most fun to play." The well-received movie earned over $100 million at the box office.

That same year, Hawn auditioned for a role in Woody Allen's musical *Everyone Says I Love You.* Allen, who didn't know she could sing, was impressed when she belted out her song at the tryout. He came over to her and said, "Oh God, you really have a voice." Hawn had kept that talent on hold for decades.

In 1997 Hawn made her debut as a director in the film *Hope.* The film is based on the 1962 Cuban missile crisis, a time when the U.S. and Russian super-powers came close to nuclear war. In 1963, Goldie had written a short story on the subject. "It was the first time I realized we could all die," Hawn says. In 1994 screenwriter Kerry Kennedy submitted a script similar to Hawn's own story. Goldie took the project idea to the cable network TNT, at the same time offering herself as director. Hawn says she was happy with the outcome of the film. However, directing is not really for her because, as Goldie says, "I love being spontaneous. When you're directing, you have to be there all the time."

Not surprisingly Hawn's latest films have been comedies, too. In 1999 she and comic Steve Martin starred in a remake of the 1970 film *The Out-of-Towners*. She liked working with Martin because they are both "physical" comics.

In the same year, *Town and Country* was released. Hawn costars with Warren Beatty, Diane Keaton, and Gary Shandling in the movie, in which a leading New York architect faces a series of choices about his life and marriage. Keaton, who has starred with Hawn in other films, is a big fan and speaks of Goldie with high praise. "The public responds to Goldie," Keaton says. "She has a lovability that's rare. . . . There's only a handful of people who are adored, and Goldie is one of them."

Hawn radiates a "lovability" not only to people but also to animals. In a 1996 PBS special, *In the Wild*, she hosted an episode entitled "The Elephants of India with Goldie Hawn." In the program, Hawn takes a train from Delhi to Jaipur, searching for a blind elephant that she had seen in the wild seven years earlier. Hawn and her crew members had to "rough it" as they ventured into the wilds of India.

Maybe one of the reasons Hawn has this great capacity for caring is her love of life. She thrives on

Hawn stars opposite Steve Martin in The Out-of-Towners.

growing and learning. "I love to wake up and meet the day. I think that life is not to be wasted or thrown away," says Hawn. Her next project is to travel around the world and search for joy. She wants to know where joy lives and to remind people that it's out there. She plans to film the experience as well. She would interview scientists, religious leaders, and heads of state. She wants to look into the biology and chemistry of the human brain and try to access a level of happiness within us. She wants to know exactly what makes people happy.

Does Goldie ever get depressed? She says that she does cry a lot. But she has researched and learned that crying actually elevates the body's immune system. In fact, according to Hawn, crying has the same effect as laughter. If you remain in a state of low-level melancholy, it brings your immune system down. Releasing emotions of any kind is really good for you, she believes.

What else does Goldie, now in her fifties, believe is important to do to keep healthy and fit? When Hawn turned 50 in 1995, she took a look at herself. After deciding that her backside could be firmer, she hired an exercise coach. Now she routinely leg presses 105 pounds, bikes around the neighborhood, and swims. She likes to crosstrain. She rides her bike up the mountain one day and uses the stairclimber the next, then works out on the running machine another day, and takes a power walk the next. Though she says she doesn't dance as much as she used to, she still stays in shape. She has a perfectly toned body. She stays fit through daily workouts with a personal trainer in a state-of-the-art gym at her Los Angeles home. The discipline of dance no doubt has helped her dedicate so much time to all the workouts.

Hawn says she works out because she wants to feel good. According to the star, many people start working out because they want to look beautiful. But that, she says, is not the right reason for exercising. She believes that working out gives people a stronger and quicker mind and body, and it makes everyone feel healthy.

Goldie's diet also reflects her desire for healthy living: she likes to drink a green mixture of spinach, kale, parsley, and any other favorite fresh vegetables. She sometimes adds apple, for sweetener, and ginger and mint to give taste to the beverage. She tries to drink it twice a day. Hawn also sticks to a diet free of wheat, sugar, and dairy products.

Goldie Hawn maintains good health through regular exercise and a positive attitude.

Goldie Hawn has been nominated for and won numerous awards over the years. She won an Oscar and a Golden Globe Award in 1969 for her role in *Cactus Flower*. She was nominated in 1980 for an Oscar for Best Actress for *Private Benjamin*. In 1981 she won the People's Choice Award for Favorite Motion Picture Actress. In 1997 she won the Blockbuster Entertainment Award for Favorite Actress in a Comedy.

In March of 1999, she won a top honor at Harvard: the Hasty Pudding Theatrical Woman of the Year Award. Hasty Pudding is a theatrical club that is more than 200 years old. The award is given to performers who have made a "lasting and impressive contribution to the world of entertainment." In past years, the prize has been awarded to Julia Roberts, Sigourney Weaver, and Lauren Bacall.

The festivities for handing out the Hasty Pudding award began with Hawn leading a parade through the streets. At the awards ceremony, the male students were dressed in women's clothing, a newer tradition for the club. At the end of the evening, Hawn was go-go dancing as she did in her younger days. The fun ended with Hawn being sprayed with Silly String and giving some advice to college seniors. "I don't know what I'm going to do now," Hawn said, "and I don't want to know. It's more fun not to know."

Hawn is used to giving advice, especially on joy and laughter. She was once quoted as saying, "Once you laugh at your own weaknesses, you can move forward. Comedy breaks down walls. It opens up people. If you're good, you can fill up those openings with something positive. Maybe you can combat the ugliness in the world."

Chronology

1945   Born November 21 to Edward Rutledge Hawn and Laura Speinhoff Hawn in Takoma Park, Maryland (a suburb of Washington D.C.)

1968   Appears as the giggly blonde in Rowan and Martin's *Laugh -In*

1969   Marries choreographer and director Gus Trikonis

1969   Wins Oscar for Best Supporting Actress for role in *Cactus Flower*

1974   Divorces Gus Trikonis

1976   Marries Bill Hudson; son Oliver Hudson is born

1979   Divorces Bill Hudson

1980   Produces and stars in *Private Benjamin*

1983   Becomes companion of Kurt Russell

1986   Son Wyatt Russell is born

1997   Makes film directing debut in *Hope*, a TNT production

1999   Stars in remake of *The Out-of-Towners*

Filmography

1968   *The One and Only, Genuine, Original Family Band*

1969   *Cactus Flower*

1970   *There's a Girl in My Soup*

1971   *$ (Dollars)*

1972   *Butterflies are Free*

1974   *The Girl from Petrovka*

1974   *The Sugarland Express*

1975   *Shampoo*

1976   *The Duchess and the Dirtwater Fox*

1978   *Foul Play*
1978   *Travels with Anita*
1979   *Lovers and Liars*
1980   *Private Benjamin*
1980   *Seems Like Old Times*
1982   *Best Friends*
1984   *Protocol*
1984   *Swing Shift*
1986   *Wildcats*
1987   *Overboard*
1990   *Bird on a Wire*
1991   *Deceived*
1992   *Crisscross*
1992   *Death Becomes Her*
1992   *Housesitter*
1996   *Everyone Says I Love You*
1996   *The First Wives Club*
1999   *The Out-of-Towners*

Television

1967–73   *Rowan and Martin's Laugh-In* (series)
1967–68   *Good Morning, World*
1970   *Pure Goldie* (host)
1978   *The Goldie Hawn Special* (host)
1980   *Goldie and Liz Together* (special)
1982   *Goldie and the Kids . . . Listen to Us* (special; host and executive producer)
1987   *Scared Sexless* (movie)
1990   *An Evening with Bette, Cher, Goldie, Meryl, Olivia, Lily, and Ro* (special)
1993   *Here's Looking at You, Warner Brothers* (special; host)

The fit and feminine Lucy Lawless

CHAPTER FOUR
Lucy Lawless

"La, la, la, la, la" is the familiar battle cry heard throughout the Amazon camp. Who is this 5' 10" blue-eyed beauty riding horseback through the wild? Who is this leather-clad avenger flashing her mighty sword as she carries out justice? The answer is Xena, Amazon warrior princess, played by New Zealand actor Lucy Lawless.

Known to millions of television viewers in more than 60 countries around the world, this heroine of a 2,000-year old tribe resides in ancient Scythia, land of the Amazon women. She travels through imaginary ancient lands, fighting to protect the powerless. Xena has become a cult figure and feminist icon to viewers worldwide. The sword-wielding heroine was such an instant hit that she was featured on the cover of *Ms.* magazine during the show's first season in 1995. Lucy Lawless describes her character as "a woman as strong as any man or woman ever has been, who lives by her wits, but is a fighter. She's a very human hero, who knows all about the darker side of human nature since she must battle within herself every day."

For the Auckland native, "girl power" began at an early age. Born Lucille Frances Ryan to Irish-Catholic parents Frank and Julie Ryan, Lucy grew up with a homemaker mother and a father who at one time was mayor of Mount Albert, Auckland. Lucy is the fifth of seven children and the older of the two girls in her family. With four older brothers to contend with, she developed into a tomboy. "I have five brothers and one sister, and my mom said I didn't know I was a girl until I was eight," she laughs. Her mother tells a story about coming around a corner one day to find her daughter chanting "Got to be a strong girl, got to be a strong girl."

Interestingly, Lucy was not an athletic child. She was always physical but, according to her, "with no finesse." Classmates at school nicknamed her "Unco," which means "uncoordinated." "I couldn't hit a ball with a bat," she claims. From the ages of 8 to 13 years old, she seldom participated in any sports, except for riding horses. What a contrast to the character she now plays, one who demonstrates enduring physical strength.

Lucy's interest in acting began when she was eight. She appeared in numerous musicals and plays in her school days. Most of her education took place in Catholic schools in New Zealand: she attended Wesley Intermediate and Marist Sisters College. At one time Lucy actually thought of becoming a marine biologist or pathologist. However, at age 17 she enrolled in Auckland University to study opera and foreign languages (French, Italian, and German). She later gave up her studies when she realized she didn't have the passion for opera.

When Lucy dropped out of college, she and boyfriend Garth Lawless traveled to Germany. For a while, the two of them earned money picking grapes along the Rhine River. Then they headed off to another adventure in Australia.

The two ended up in Kalgoorlie, a small town located five hundred miles from Perth. Kalgoorlie is a gold-mining town. Lucy found work there doing all sorts of jobs, such as digging, mapping, and driving trucks. She was one of the few women able to do the same difficult work as the men. As she explains, the idea of gold mining being glamorous is nothing but a myth: "I know some people have a romantic image of carrying a canary in a gold mine, but it's simply not true." Lucy says her adventure included running through the Australian outback away from the area being blasted. Then she and other miners would run back to the detonation site and retrieve samples. Lucy was very isolated during this time. She was living in the Outback with a cat called Basil, kangaroos, and emus. She and her boyfriend Garth wouldn't see anybody for weeks at a time.

Lucy and Garth Lawless married in Australia and soon afterward moved back to Auckland, where their daughter, Daisy, was born. At that time Lucy began to actively pursue a career in acting. She made several commercials. In her first commercial, she wore a bathing suit. Lawless laughs at this, saying, "And I wasn't a bathing suit girl." That job, however, led to other commercials. At age 20, Lucy got her first acting job. She performed with a comedy troupe on television called *Funny Business*.

Soon afterwards, she moved to Vancouver, Canada, with her husband and baby, to study acting at the William Davies Center for Actors. Garth worked as a bar manager at the time. Eight months later, in early 1992, Lucy and family moved back to New Zealand. There she started work as a cohost for *Air New Zealand Holiday,* a travel magazine show. The show, broadcast in New Zealand, took her around the world.

Other television opportunities opened up for Lucy in 1992. She played Liddy Barton in the episode "Fee Fie Foe Fum" of *Ray Bradbury Theater*. She played Sarah McFee in *The Black Stallion*. She also appeared in the television movie *Rainbow Warrior*, which was about the French sinking a Greenpeace ship in New Zealand waters. In 1993, she played Mink Tertius in the miniseries *Typhon's People*. That same year she played Chloe Miller in *Marlin Bay*.

Lawless first guest-starred on *Hercules: The Legendary Journeys* in 1992 as Lyla, Deric the Centaur's courageous young bride. Two years later she appeared as the menacing Amazon Lysia in the two-hour action-packed television movie *Hercules and the Amazon Women*.

The role of Xena originated in 1995, in a three-part episode of *Hercules: The Legendary Journeys*. Vanessa Angel was originally cast as Xena, but she became ill and could not take the part. Four others were offered the role, but they turned it down because none of them wanted to miss the Hollywood pilot season. They were also reluctant to go to far-off New Zealand, where the show is filmed. Perhaps most important, they were probably afraid to try an unproved show. Lawless, though, readily accepted the opportunity.

The three episodes ultimately led to the spin-off show *Xena: Warrior Princess*. "God bless them," Lucy laughs, thinking of the four actors who could have had her role. "Never in my wildest dreams did I ever think I'd one day be a female action hero. I thought I'd be doing Shakespeare." Not only did Lawless get a role of a lifetime but she would also meet her second husband Robert Tapert, the show's executive producer, on the set.

Lawless as a cult figure and feminist icon in Xena.

The show was launched in 1995. Soon afterwards, Lucy divorced her husband, Garth, but she kept her married name. She joked that she had once thought of using the name Rita Reckless instead. She now feels that she couldn't have come up with a better name than Lawless for someone who plays a warrior princess. Her admiring fans often refer to her as "Flawless," taking the "F" from her middle name, Frances, and attaching it to her married name.

Xena: Warrior Princess got overwhelmingly positive reviews from the critics. They clearly appreciated the show's retelling of ancient history and imaginative weaving of mythological tales. The program became so popular that soon every kind of product promoting it was available. The current merchandise includes Xena apparel, comic books, magazines, trading cards, and jewelry. The first official Xena convention was held in January 1997 in the United States. Many other fan get-togethers occur around the globe. At the Albacon Sci-Fi convention in Glasgow, Scotland, many Xena followers were in attendance. In July 1997 Lawless teamed up with *Hercules* star Kevin Sorboto to open a new attraction at Universal Studios in Florida. There is also a Xena race car on the NASCAR circuit, driven by NASCAR's only female driver, Patty Moise. The show has even inspired the creation of college classes entitled "Xena 101."

When Xena was first introduced to television viewers, she was not the heroine fans know and love today. She started out as a bad character—as Lawless describes her, "a woman with the devil on her shoulder, who is constantly fighting the darker side of her own nature." Circumstances in the show reformed Xena. She rethought her evil ways and became the heroine the world admires today.

The once uncoordinated Lawless stays in top physical condition.

The show attracts many viewers for a variety of reasons. Lawless believes that one appeal is that people identify with the character—Xena has struggled and overcome her inner weaknesses. The heroine now battles giants, monsters, and a variety of other evil characters. Another appeal is the imagination of the story lines. The plots have a variety of moods. They can be dark and serious or very comedic in a slapstick sort of way. The production is also enhanced by its spectacular setting, the outdoor film locations in and around Auckland. Sets are constructed in a series of industrial estates in West Auckland. They consist of temples, barns, ice caverns, and labyrinths, which are built and then quickly torn down. Yet another aspect of the show's appeal is the exotic costuming of both the Amazons and their foes.

Lawless had dropped the horseback riding of her childhood days, but she picked it up again when she started the Xena series. Her role is intensely physical and tough. Lucy does her own fighting and riding scenes in the outdoor film locations in Auckland. She claims her job has forced her to develop quick reflexes. As Xena, she has had to endure punches and even once a black eye. Fitness is essential for the role of the warrior princess.

In 1997 *Xena: Warrior Princess* was one of the highest rated syndicated programs. Lawless says she thinks her character is appealing because of her strong nature. She also feels the show's popularity is due mainly to the main character, who carries the message "Yes, I can" in both her actions and demeanor. That means "Yes, I can alone," with no help from men. On the other hand, Lawless thinks many men view the Xena character as someone they'd like to sit with and have a beer. This is a bit of a surprise since in many episodes the male characters are often cut down to size by Xena's mighty sword. Or in other cases she faces off with male warriors in hand-to-hand combat. One male character who did get revenge was a Roman soldier who broke Xena's leg in one episode. The soldier was played by Lawless's brother Daniel Ryan.

The star often works a 12-hour day filled with reading scripts, learning fight sequences, having wardrobe fittings, and meeting with the public. She is also kept busy signing autographs and attending publicity and charity events.

Lawless is very involved with her family, too. She shares custody of Daisy with Garth Lawless. Daisy spends weekends with her father and weekdays with her mother. On March 28, 1998, Lucy Lawless married the show's executive producer, Robert Tapert in Santa Monica, California. In 1999 Lawless became pregnant with her second child. During her pregnancy, Renaissance Pictures, which produces the show, continued to film the show, creatively hiding Lawless's condition for the season. Her son, Julius Robert Bay Tapert, was born in October 1999.

What does it take to play the warrior princess? For Lawless, a change of hair color was the first requirement. Her natural hair color is ash blonde. She also has a porcelain-white complexion but for the show is sponged down in brown makeup to give her a tanned and rugged appearance. The effect, which takes about five minutes to put on, takes a lot longer to remove.

And of course Lawless must be in top physical shape. She has been trained in the martial arts by master Douglas Wong (*Dragon: The Bruce Lee Story*), who taught Lawless basic kung fu moves. She can now fight with swords and staffs, and she keeps a sword in her car trunk to practice her moves when she can. Lawless enjoys the punches and the high kicks that occur during the fight scenes. However, in the action scenes, she doesn't do backflips or reverses. Although most of what the viewer sees is Lawless, but if only the back of Xena's head is seen, it's a stand-in for Lawless. Lucy states, "I've now reached a stage where I feel fitter and a lot more at home with the physical demands of the role. . . I do all the fights unless we don't have time or it's considered too dangerous."

So, what does Lawless have to do to keep up with the physical demands of her job as Xena, the warrior princess? First of all, she has to eat right. For her diet, the 140-pound Lucy says she likes to eat baked beans, chili, soy milk, and eggs. She tries to avoid dairy products. Unfortunately, one of her favorite foods, besides lamb shanks, is frozen yogurt.

To tone her body, Lawless joined Pilates Body Studio in Auckland, where she fits three 90-minute sessions a week into her busy schedule. As a result of this training, she says she now has better flexibility and posture and a firmer abdomen. Her muscles are toned and she has the line and length of a dancer and a sense of being even taller than she actually is. Lawless states that the workouts have also made her more confident physically. Working out regularly at the Pilates Body Studio has increased her stamina and flexibility. Lawless notes, "My kicks at work have been a lot higher and freer." Other goals of her fitness routines are to tone her legs and keep her knees strong.

Lucy says the workouts at Pilates have also toned her legs and shoulders. According to *New Zealand Fitness Magazine*, she is "all line, length, and lean muscle."

Relaxing at home

Readers of the magazine recently chose Lawless as number one in its "Best Bodies" poll. She claims she is hooked on the Pilates body conditioning program, which strives to improve body awareness through improving coordination and stamina.

Of course, even a heroine has to have her relaxation time. Lawless enjoys listening to music, noting that her favorite pop artists include Lyle Lovett, Lenny Kravitz, Annie Lennox, Etta James, and Tuck and Patti. Her favorite old-time performers are jazz clarinetist Benny Goodman and singer Peggy Lee. Lawless's favorite film actor is Susan Sarandon. Other interests include watching science fiction films and reading books on psychology. To relax Lucy practices yoga. She also enjoys being out in nature. She says she'd love to rollerblade, although she says she's not very good at it. She and husband Rob Tapert love to go fishing. Recently she has begun to play golf. Lawless is also an ice hockey fan and a big supporter of the Detroit Red Wings.

In addition to being a cult figure for women around the world, Lawless is also a role model. Lawless states, "I quit smoking for instance because I don't want young women who look up to me to think it's OK." However, the idea of being a role model did make her a bit uncomfortable at first. "It was very disconcerting. But eventually I came to see it can be really pleasant, that people aren't expecting more of me just that I be human."

In 1998 *People* magazine included Lawless on three of its honorary lists: "50 Most Beautiful People in the World," "TV's Most Fascinating Stars," and "25 Most Intriguing People of the Year." That same year she was awarded the New Zealand Entertainer of the Year

Award, as well as the Award for International Achievement.

What brought Lawless to this point of success in her life? Basically, she is a natural optimist. She has always believed she'd succeed. "I've always had this unbelievable faith in myself, to the point of arrogance," she says. However, despite having achieved fame worldwide, she is considered to be very down-to-earth and friendly. Lucy claims that in New Zealand being normal is no big deal. She says that it's not in the national character to get carried away with yourself.

Despite her talent and optimism, Lawless has faced some setbacks. In 1996 she fell off a horse while performing a stunt on *The Tonight Show*. Lucy's horse slipped and fell on the concrete, and Lucy hit the pavement. She broke her pelvis in four places. Lawless says the best thing about the accident was that it made her stop and think, and be able to put her fears in order. "It made me realize what's really important," she says.

Lawless is very honest when discussing an emotional breakdown she had in 1998. At the time, she had been involved in a grueling multi-episode of *Xena* that was being shot during a period of bad weather. For months, the star had been working in snow and rain. Eventually, she began to have a neural association, that is, she began to associate work with physical discomfort. She was constantly thinking about how much pain she was in, and she dreaded going to work every day. This situation became especially difficult to handle because she is married to the show's producer. Luckily, Lawless got some self-help tapes and pulled herself out of this mental difficulty.

She says now that the job helps her keep her head on straight and that she appreciates her crew, who

Lucy is a natural optimist.

work hard long hours and love their work. She says they are her inspiration because of their dedication to the job that they do. "I've come to see that practicing appreciation and gratitude is the way to health and happiness," explains Lawless.

Lawless also appreciates the woman who plays Xena's loyal companion on the show, Gabrielle. Lawless notes that Texan actor Renee O'Connor is "the woman I most love to work with in the world." Naturally both actors have to abandon their accents for the flat mid-American voices the television characters use. However, Lawless is used to working with accents. She tries to keep up with her earlier studies of foreign languages. She is now reviewing her earlier study of German.

And where did Xena's famous battle cry come from? The producers of the show had wanted her to mimic a kind of Arabic sound called an ululation. When she couldn't master an ululation, she adopted a variation of the warble. Fortunately, she is able to do this loudly, without hurting her throat.

That's good news because Lawless has also had a chance to use her musical talents on the stage. Her start in Broadway theater began accidentally. Once, Lawless appeared on *The Rosie O'Donnell Show,* where she sang "I'm an Old Cowhand." Afterwards Lucy and Rosie had a conversation that drifted to a discussion about the 1950s musical *Grease* and one of its characters, a tough-talking woman named Rizzo. O'Donnell commented that she had played the Rizzo character herself. Watching the show at the time were the producers of the *Grease* musical playing on Broadway. They liked what they heard and offered Lawless an opportunity to play Rizzo.

The Broadway run took place during September and October of 1997 during a break from the filming of *Xena: Warrior Princess*. Lucy followed in the footsteps of Brooke Shields as well as Rosie O'Donnell in the role of Rizzo. Lawless received great reviews from the critics. She also received plenty of flowers from fans. She was especially pleased that many fans also sent donations in her name to Daytop Village, a drug treatment facility she supports. The theater was packed during Lawless's performance in the musical *Grease,* and she says she would definitely like to work again on the stage.

Lawless has appeared in more recent films as well. In 1997 she made a brief appearance as herself in the film *Something So Right.* That same year her voice was used yet again as Xena in the animated movie *Hercules and Xena: The Battle for Mount Olympus.* Her latest movie role was a cameo appearance in 1998 in the movie *I'll Make You Happy.*

Lawless definitely has a lot to keep her busy. She intends to pursue movie work when Xena ends its run. For now, plans are for the show to continue at least until 2001. However, Lucy is careful to make one point: "Career is not as important as having a long successful marriage and having more kids. If I had to choose, I'd go for the family over Oscars any day. If I didn't, I'd kick myself when I'm 80." Lawless is presently living in Auckland, New Zealand, with her husband, daughter, son, and a couple of dogs. Her parents live nearby.

Chronology

1968 Born Lucille Frances Ryan on March 29, 1968, to Frank and Julie Ryan in Mount Albert, Auckland, New Zealand

1986 Enrolls in Auckland University to study opera and Italian, French, and German languages

1988 Marries high school sweetheart, Garth Lawless

1989 Daughter Daisy Lawless is born

1989 Lands first acting job on television with a comedy troupe called *Funny Business;* studies acting in Vancouver at the William Davis Center for Actors Study

1994 Stars as *Xena: Warrior Princess*

1995 Divorces Garth Lawless

1996 Fractures her pelvis when thrown from a horse while preparing for a skit for *The Tonight Show with Jay Leno*

1998 Marries Robert Tapert, executive producer of *Xena,* on March 28

1999 Son Julius Robert Bay Tapert is born

Television

1992 *The Rainbow Warrior* (movie special)

1993 *Typhon's People* (mini-series)

1992 *The Ray Bradbury Theater* (episode)

1994 *Hercules and the Amazon Women* (movie special)

1995 *Hercules: The Legendary Journeys* (appearance)

1995 *Xena: Warrior Princess* (series)

1998 *Hercules and Xena—The Animated Movie: The Battle for Mount Olympus* (voice)

Demi Moore is a successful actress, mother, and businesswoman.

CHAPTER FIVE
Demi Moore

Demi Moore has learned to overcome great adversity in her life. At the same time she has also learned how to set goals and work hard to achieve them. "I have always worked," she says. "When I think of these people who need to be encouraged, and they're sitting there floundering, I can't relate to it. I can't imagine a life that wasn't about setting goals and accomplishing things."

Many people consider Demi Moore an ideal mother and a shrewd businesswoman. She has three daughters whom she adores and is one of the highest-paid actors in Hollywood. In a 1992 interview with *Vanity Fair* magazine, Moore is quoted as saying, "I just want the end result of things to be the highest quality they can be. I want good work. I want things to be the best they can be. I want greatness." Moore is relentless in her drive to achieve her goals. However, life was not always as glamorous for Moore as it is today. But it is likely that her tough beginning gave her the ambition to be the successful woman she has become.

Demi Moore was born Demetria Gene Guynes on November 11, 1962, in Roswell, New Mexico. Her parents were Danny and Virginia Guynes. According to Demi, her mother picked her baby's name out of a beauty magazine. Demi says she doesn't know whether she was named after a hair product or makeup. Her parents married and divorced twice. She grew up with her younger half-brother Morgan, born in 1967, who today works as a film technician.

Demi's early years were quite unstable. Her family moved 30 times before she was a teenager. Her father, who worked as a newspaper ad man, constantly moved the family in search of work. Often the moves were also a way to escape Danny Guynes's debts. The moves made it difficult for Demi to establish and maintain friendships. "I never went to less than two schools in a year," Demi says. "I just tried to assimilate as fast as possible. What that's given me is a gift to assess situations and people. It makes you adaptable. The downside is you never really get an understanding of how you build a relationship."

Life was difficult enough, but to complicate matters, at age 12 Demi developed a crossed right eye that required two operations to correct. Then, at age 14, she suffered a tremendous emotional blow. She discovered that Danny Guynes, the man that she had grown up with, was not her biological father. She had been conceived in 1962 during her mother's two-month marriage to a soldier in the U.S. Air Force. Years later Demi would meet her biological father, but she says she has no relationship with him now.

The young teen suffered from a difficult family life. Her parents were constantly drinking and fighting. Demi says of this period, "I got lost. I had an essence in my life that I was nothing." Finally, when Demi was about 13, Danny and Virginia Guynes' marriage ended and her mother eventually moved the rest of the family to California. Further tragedy would follow five years later, when Danny Guynes would commit suicide by inhaling carbon monoxide from his car's exhaust pipe. The newspaper tabloids have made headlines out of many of her parents' early troubles, but Demi doesn't dwell on these problems. She actually speaks kindly of her mother and father, "They gave me a lot of good things, and I truly believe they did the best they could."

In Los Angeles, California, Demi attended Fairfax High School, but she dropped out at age 16. She essentially began her adult life then. She leased an apartment, started work at a debt collection agency, and obtained some modeling jobs. When she was 18, she met her future husband, Freddy Moore, at a nightclub in Los Angeles. Moore was a guitarist in a rock band. Their marriage would last four years.

During her marriage to the rock musician, Demi Moore's career took an unexpected turn. She and her husband were living next door to an aspiring, German actor named Nastassja Kinski. The young woman asked Moore for help in practicing lines from scripts. The experience sparked an acting interest in Moore, and she enrolled in some drama classes. In 1982, although she had little acting experience, Demi beat out 1,000 other women for a role on the daytime television soap opera *General Hospital*. She soon became a big hit on the show, enjoying her own fan club and receiving a substantial income. As another actor from the show would note, "[Demi] had street smarts. She learned fast." She purchased a home in West Hollywood, where she lived with her mother and brother after ending her marriage to Freddy Moore.

In 1983 Moore left *General Hospital* to work on the film *Blame It on Rio*, which was unsuccessful at the box office. Her big break came a year later, though, when

Demi appeared on General Hospital for a while with Tony Geary.

she was cast as a coke addict in the 1984 film *St. Elmo's Fire*. Ironically, at that time Moore had actually developed her own drug and alcohol problem. When the director learned of her addiction, he threatened to fire her. Fortunately Moore, with the help of a rehabilitation center, was able to clean up her act in two weeks. She became clean and sober and since then has never looked back. After that experience, Moore focused on her career and became the success she is today.

Moore's body has always been an important asset. The 5' 5" Demi has worked hard to achieve and maintain top physical condition. She says that she has always loved working out and has made a commitment to herself that she didn't want to look and feel good just for a movie, but for herself. She sees the long-term value of taking care of her own body. "When I see 70-year-olds going out hiking, I want that. It takes discipline and hard work, but to me that represents a truly rich life, to be able to give that to yourself."

In 1986 Moore turned to acting on the stage. She appeared in the off-Broadway production of *The Early Girl*. Her role was Lily, the new girl at a bordello in a western mining town. The *New York Times* noted that she made a "striking stage debut." Surely her well-known husky voice was an asset for the role.

During the next few years Moore made several films that were not as well received by critics. At the time she was known as belonging to a circle of popular, young actors referred to as the Brat Pack. One of the members of the pack was Emilio Estevez, whom Moore dated and at one point was even engaged to off and on during 1987. Later that year she met Bruce Willis, who would become her second husband. The two met at a screening of the 1987 film *Stakeout*. After seeing each other daily over the next four months, the two decided to wed.

An impulsive decision to marry found Demi and Bruce taking their vows in Las Vegas, Nevada, before a justice of the peace. However, three weeks later they married again at an elaborate ceremony held on a Hollywood soundstage. Singer Little Richard, who is also an ordained minister, performed the marriage rites, while behind him a 30-member gospel choir, wearing black sunglasses, performed. The extravagant affair was attended by 450 friends, 12 ushers, and 12 bridesmaids. The bride and groom, who would soon become known for their high-priced lifestyle, spent $850,000 on the ceremony.

Moore had always wanted a family, and she and Willis began theirs on August 16, 1988, with the birth of a daughter, Rumer Glenn. Demi, who would gain a reputation for giving her children unusual names, named her first daughter after British novelist Rumer Godden. Her second daughter, Scout LaRue, born in 1991, was named for a character in the novel and film *To Kill a Mockingbird*.

It was during her second pregnancy with daughter Scout that Moore gained notoriety. In her seventh month of the pregnancy, Demi Moore appeared on the cover of *Vanity Fair* wearing nothing but diamonds. Her arms encircled her breasts and protruding belly. The nude photo, taken by the magazine's well-known photographer Annie Lebovitz, sparked heated debates. Some stores in the United States and Canada banned the magazine. Moore says she wouldn't have allowed herself to be photographed if she had thought it morally questionable. "I did feel glamorous, and beautiful, and more free about my body."

One reason Moore felt and looked so beautiful during her pregnancy was that she was in such top physical condition. Two days before Scout was born, Demi had taken a two-and-a-half-hour hike. Two months after her second daughter's birth, Demi was back at work, keeping to a strict workout schedule. She was jogging alongside her trainer at three in the morning before showing up on the set for her 5 A.M. call.

Not long after Scout's birth, Demi posed for another *Vanity Fair* cover, this time wearing nothing but body paint. As the photograph showed, her body was in perfect condition. For Moore, the photo publication was a great career move. She was able to show the public she was fit and ready to work again, as well as still a national sex symbol.

Moore's commitment to her career did not lessen her interest in her family life, though. She was once quoted as saying, "A family, for me as a young girl, was my image of what I hoped for. It was part of the big picture." In 1994, Moore and husband Willis expanded their family to include a third daughter, Tallulah Belle.

In between having children, Moore was also busy making films. Her big breakthrough came in 1990 when she appeared with Patrick Swayze in the film *Ghost*. The movie tells a love story about a murdered New York investment banker, played by Swayze and his grieving artist girlfriend, played by Moore. After her boyfriend's death, a spiritualist, played by Whoopi Goldberg, acts as an intermediary between the dead man's ghost and love. Romantics around the world adored *Ghost*, and the film made millions of dollars at the box office. At 28-years-old, with a signature single tear running down her cheek, *Ghost*'s Demi Moore skyrocketed to stardom. She was now on Hollywood's A-list.

Success enabled Moore in 1991 to start her own production company in Santa Monica, California, along with Suzanne and Jennifer Todd. The company name, Rufglen, was changed because it proved too difficult to pronounce; Moore later changed it to Moving Pictures. Some of the films Demi has produced over the years are *Mortal Thoughts* (1991), *Now and Then* (1995), *If These Walls Could Talk* (1996), *Austin Powers: International Man of Mystery* (1997), and *G.I. Jane* (1997).

And just where did the name Rufglen come from? It was the name of an imaginary place her grandmother had made up. "Rufglen was like a fairy tale," Moore explains. "The mental image was . . . like small castle walls, but not a castle inside. Inside it was cozier and more like a cottage in a forest." Demi has fond memories of her grandmother. Before her family had moved to California, Demi had lived with her maternal grandmother for a few months. There Demi had experienced domestic stability for the first time. Her grandmother was a strong personality who provided for her disabled husband and four children. Years later Moore would identify her grandmother as one of the individuals who most influenced her life. Moore would even contribute a section describing her grandmother to a 1997 book called *Pearls of Wisdom from Grandma*.

Besides cofounding the new production company in 1991, Demi Moore also became involved in another project. In partnership with husband Bruce Willis and with actors Sylvester Stallone and Arnold Schwarzenegger, she opened a chain of flashy Planet Hollywood International Restaurants. The eateries are located throughout the United States and in many countries worldwide. However, the chain later did not prove successful, and as the worth of the company's stock declined, several restaurants were forced to shut their doors.

Moore also starred in a few not so memorable films in 1991 before coming up with another hit in 1992. That year she starred as Lieutenant Commander Joanne Galloway in *A Few Good Men*. To get in shape for the role of Galloway, Demi hired a full-time personal trainer. It was the final three months of her second pregnancy, and she started on a regimen of pool exercises, knowing she would have to be in shape to be back at work in two months. After Scout's birth, Demi began an exercise routine in which she put in three hours of training a day. Her exercise program included biking, hiking, running, and weight-resistance training—all undertaken to ensure proper muscle-building and body chiseling.

In 1993 Moore starred in the controversial film *Indecent Proposal*. In the movie she plays a married woman, Diane Murphy, who agrees to sleep with a wealthy stranger for one night in exchange for a million dollars. In *Disclosure* (1994) she plays a female sexual harasser. However, perhaps her most controversial film was *Striptease* (1996), based on a novel by Carl Hiaasen. Moore plays a unemployed mother caught in a custody battle who decides to make money for a court appeal by stripping at a club. Before filming began, Moore researched a great deal of background material to find out how her character should be played, including thoroughly reading the novel and spending months in stripbars.

Then of course Moore had to ensure that her body was in top condition to play the role. Her daily exercise routine incorporated an early morning run on the beach, up to three hours of dance rehearsal, two and a half hours of yoga, and a session with her personal trainer in a special trailer containing $15,000 worth of gym equipment. After completing filming, Demi promoted *Striptease* by appearing on the *Late Show with David Letterman* wearing only a bikini and cards with the host's infamous top-ten list taped all over her body. Moore, who in 1993 had been described by Letterman as "the most successful actress working today," made an even greater impression on Letterman at this appearance.

For her performance in *Striptease,* Moore received 12.5 million dollars, an amount that made her the highest paid actress in movie history. Certainly such high earnings allow her to enjoy an extravagant lifestyle, for which she has become well-known. Moore loves flying in private jets; coworkers relate how much she enjoys flying on the studios' private planes. She is also able to afford to hire numerous assistants and has a staff that includes bodyguards, nannies for her children, household workers, a cook, a hairdresser, a makeup artist, and of course—the essential for every celebrity—the personal trainer.

In 1996 Moore was busy on a much tamer project than usual—in the animated film *The Hunchback of Notre Dame,* produced by Walt Disney Pictures. Her husky voice is that of the film's heroine, Esmeralda.

Yet another film, released in 1997, once again showed off Moore's highly conditioned physique. Only this time the role wasn't that of a sexy bombshell. This time she was Lieutenant Jordan O'Neil in *G.I. Jane.* For her fictional role as the first female candidate for the elite Combined Reconnaissance Team who must undergo training as a Navy SEAL, Demi had to be in top condition. Navy SEALs undergo the toughest physical training there is in the U.S. military, although Moore's character also has to battle the resentment of her male peers.

At the time of the film's release, Moore said of the role, "I hope that it offers a positive vision for women, especially those women who might say, 'I'd like to do that, but I'd never make the grade.'" Moore elaborates on why it was important to get in top physical shape for the film: "I needed to create an accurate and appropriate physical image for Jordan O'Neil. I didn't want to be superbuff like a bodybuilder. I just wanted to be believable, and to make sure that the audience didn't look at me onscreen and think, "That's ridiculous, that little spindly person punching someone out."

During the filming of *G.I. Jane,* Moore worked almost entirely on a male set. She liked hanging out with the men and being "one of the boys." She trained with them and, although she herself doesn't drink, sat up late in bars with them.

Demi's part required her to undergo grueling Special Forces training with a team of former SEALs. First she shaved her head to make herself more aquadynamic. Then she learned to do one-arm push-ups, a stunt she repeated on another appearance of the Letterman show. And she underwent "surf torture," a process that involved floating motionless in near-freezing seawater for hours at a time. In the film, Moore lugs landing craft around with the team, and she suffers tendinitis, jungle rot, and menstrual cramps. She also has to deal with a brutal drill sergeant. In one scene of the movie, he punches Moore in the stomach to demonstrate how the enemy would treat her after capture. Moore's character slugs him back and is forced to realize what she has to do to succeed.

Demi had to be in top physical shape to play Lt. Jordan O'Neil in G.I. Jane.

For so many of Moore's films, she has had to work and rework her body. She says her motivations for having done so have much to do with standard female insecurity. As she explains, it is just that she is like many other women who are trying to work out answers to body image issues.

When asked once how her relationship with her body evolved, she replied, "From total self-hate." This response is shocking, considering how Moore's body has been such a focal point of her success. She says that she has worked hard to overcome these negative feelings. She also notes that the majority of women have a distorted body image and that sometimes she is a victim of it. As Demi explains, she has received as much negative attention for being heavy as she has for being in shape.

In addition to dedicating much of her time to developing the optimum body shape, Moore is constantly trying to advance her education. Perhaps because of dropping out of school at a young age, she is very sensitive about not knowing very much about books and authors. She strives to overcome this and says, "It's like I say to my kids all the time: To not know is the most exciting thing, because then you get to know."

Despite Moore's insecurity, producer Sherry Lansing of *Indecent Proposal* describes Demi as "one of the smartest people I've ever met." Rob Reiner, director of *A Few Good Men*, would surely concur. Reiner commented, "She projects intelligence, she is intelligent."

When filming of *G.I. Jane* was over, Moore felt a little burned out on her exercise routine. In 1997 the star claimed that she was still a big believer in the importance and value of exercise. However, she toned down her exercise plan because the goal of obtaining the highly muscular body type of a military officer was no longer required.

Many of the roles that Moore has played in films like *G.I. Jane* and *A Few Good Men* are tough characters who rarely smile. This is fine with Moore, who is known not to like to smile in front of the camera. Despite this cool presence in films, colleagues comment that Moore actually has a childlike quality. Rosie O'Donnell, who costarred with Demi in the film *Now and Then,* once commented, "She likes to have sleepovers: she goes to Toys 'R' Us and buys a thousand dollars' worth of toys for the kids on the set." And her daughter Rumer said, "Whenever we go to Toys 'R' Us, I get to buy a doll, and Mommy gets to buy a doll."

Family is very important to Moore. Given her shaky upbringing, such a value is not surprising. In 1998, however, her hopes for having an intact family were shattered. In June she and Bruce Willis went public with their intention to separate. Many in Hollywood speculate that the separation probably had to do with a common problem actors face— spending too much time apart while working on film projects.

Moore now relishes the time she can spend with her own children. In 1999 she took a break from her busy schedule to devote more time to her three daughters. No doubt she will not be out of the public eye for long. More than one observer in Hollywood has noted Demi Moore's determination. She expresses it like this: "Having it all just means having the things that make you happy . . . . If I see it as possible, it is possible."

Chronology

1962   Born Demetria Gene Guynes on November 11 to Danny Guynes and Virginia King Guynes, in Roswell, New Mexico
1980   Marries musician Freddy Moore
1981   Appears in first acting role in television in the daytime soap opera drama *General Hospital*
1984   Makes her big breakthrough in film with *St. Elmo's Fire;* divorces Freddy Moore
1987   Marries actor Bruce Willis
1988   Daughter Rumer Glenn Willis is born
1991   Plays Molly Jensen in *Ghost;* nominated for a Golden Globe Award for Best Actress in a Musical or Comedy; daughter Scout La Rue Willis is born
1994   Daughter Tallulah Belle Willis is born
1996   Stars in the film *Striptease* and earns $12.5 million, making her the highest paid actress in film history
1999   Harris Poll rates Demi Moore as the most popular female movie star; separates from husband Bruce Willis

Filmography

1981   *Choices*
1982   *Parasite*
1982   *Young Doctors in Love*
1984   *Blame It on Rio*
1985   *No Small Affair*
1985   *St. Elmo's Fire*
1986   *About Last Night*
1986   *One Crazy Summer*
1986   *Wisdom*
1988   *The Seventh Sign*
1989   *We're No Angels*
1990   *Ghost*
1991   *The Butcher's Wife*
1991   *Nothing but Trouble*
1991   *Mortal Thoughts*
1992   *A Few Good Men*
1992   *Indecent Proposal*
1994   *A Century of Cinema*
1994   *Disclosure*
1995   *Now and Then*

1995	*The Scarlet Letter*	*Hiroshige*
1996	*Beavis and Butt-Head Do America*	
1996	*The Hunchback of Notre Dame*	
1996	*The Juror*	
1996	*Striptease*	
1997	*Deconstructing Harry*	
1997	*G.I. Jane*	

Television

1982–83	*General Hospital* (series)
1984	*Bedrooms* (special)
1987	*Judge Reinhold and Demi Moore in the Newcomer's Guide to Happiness* (special)
1990	*Dead Right* (special)
1996	*If These Walls Could Talk* (performer, producer)

Further Reading

Cerio, Gregory, et al. "Eye of the Tiger: Striptease's Demi Moore Knows What it Took to Get to the Top. Her Scarlet Letter is A for Ambition." People 45, no. 25 (June 24, 1996): 88.

Cher, and Robert Haas, M.S. Forever Fit: The Lifetime Plan for Health, Fitness and Beauty. New York: Bantam Books, 1991.

"Demi One of the Boys." Harper's Bazaar 4329 (August 1997): 148.

Gibson, Thomas. "Lucy Lawless, Model Citizen." TV Zone 109 (December 1998): 17.

Jerome, Jim. "Being Cher." People 49, no. 20 (May 25, 1998): 84.

Jordan, Peg. "Cher Fitness." American Fitness 10, no. 2 (March 1992): 30.

Kroll, Jack. "Survival of the Fittest." Newsweek 130, no. 8 (August 25, 1997): 73.

Krucoff, Carol. "Secrets of the Celebrity Trainers." The Saturday Evening Post (July/August 1996): 26.

"Lucy Lawless: Body Shape Secrets." American Fitness 17, no. 3 (April/May 1999): 26.

Nash, Alanna. "Solid Goldie." Good Housekeeping 225, no. 1 (July 1997): 76.

Smith, Liz. "A Heart of Goldie: Fast, fun girl talk with Goldie Hawn about female power, cheating men, and her mission to find the true source of happiness." Good Housekeeping 222, no. 4 (April 1999): 122.

Index